MIGHTY MACHINES

Stories of machines at work

KINGFISHER

NEW YORK

CONTENTS

KINGFISHER
Larousse Kingfisher Chambers Inc.
95 Madison Avenue
New York, New York 10016

First published in 2000
The material in this edition was previously
published in five individual volumes in 1990

2 4 6 8 10 9 7 5 3 1

1TR/0600/(UNI)/100IWF

LIBRARY OF CONGRESS CATALOGING-IN-PUBLICATION DATA
Royston, Angela.
Mighty machines: stories of machines at work /
by Angela Royston.—1st ed.
p. cm.
Summary: Simple stories describe various vehicles—including a digger,
a tractor, a tugboat, a helicopter, and a jet—and the work they do.
ISBN 0-7534-5315-0
1. Motor vehicles—Juvenile literature.
[1. Motor vehicles.] I. Title.

TL147 .R69 2000
629.04—dc21   00-025792

Printed in Spain

THE STORY OF A
DIGGER

The digger in this story is a JCB 3CX. It is used on all kinds of construction sites. The driver has two sets of controls, one for the loader at the front and one for the backhoe at the back.

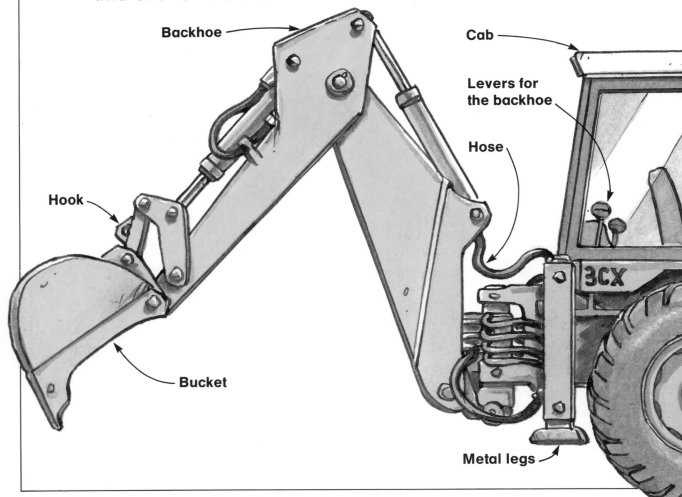

Backhoe

Cab

Levers for the backhoe

Hose

Hook

Bucket

3CX

Metal legs

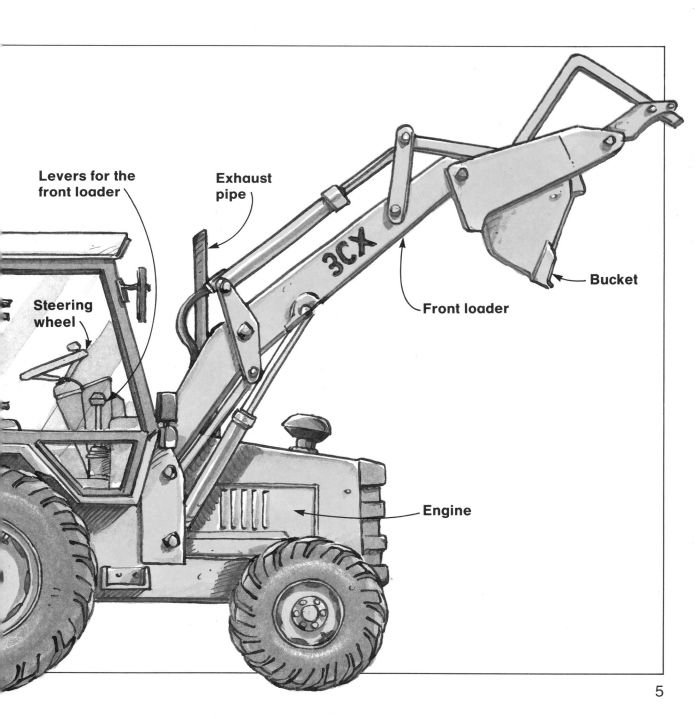

Levers for the front loader

Exhaust pipe

Steering wheel

3CX

Bucket

Front loader

Engine

5

Early one morning, a huge truck turns into the construction site. It is carrying a digger. The ramp at the back of the truck is lowered, and Pete carefully drives his digger off the truck. He looks around. Pete knows that he will have a lot to do, helping to build this new housing development.

Ed, the foreman, shows him some bumpy ground that needs to be cleared. Pete drives over and then turns his seat around so that he is facing the back of the digger. He pulls the levers to lower the metal legs that keep the digger steady while the back wheels lift off the ground.

Next, Pete pulls the levers that work the backhoe.
He makes the bucket reach out and scrape up some
rubble. Then it lifts, swings around, and drops the
rubble into a dump truck. The digger works slowly
until the ground is cleared and flat.

The next morning, Pete's job is to dig a trench for the foundation of a house. He attaches a narrow bucket to the backhoe, scoops out the soil, and drops it into the dump truck. He dumps load after load.

When Pete has finished digging, the cement mixer pours concrete into the bottom of the trench.

After the concrete has hardened, the bricklayers build a low wall on top of it.

Pete brings the digger back and fills in around the wall with the front loader. Then he makes sure that the ground is level.

The weeks pass, and more houses have to be built. One day, Pete is using the digger to clear some ground when Ed runs over. He waves his arms and shouts over the noise of the engine, "That truck is stuck in the mud. Can you pull it out?"

It has been raining hard all night, making the ground wet and muddy. The more the truck tries to move, the deeper it sinks. Pete attaches a chain from a hook on the backhoe to the truck and slowly hauls the truck out of the mud.

Pete's next job is to dig a deep trench to lay pipes for the new houses. He attaches a wide bucket to the backhoe and scoops out the soil. He dumps each load beside the trench, to put back on top of the pipes later. Suddenly, the bucket hits a big lump of rock.

"I can't move this. I'll need to break it up first,"
thinks Pete. So he takes the bucket off the backhoe
and puts on a giant breaker. The breaker roars and
shudders and quickly smashes through the rock.

When the trench is finished, it is so deep that Mike, the banksman, cannot see over the top. A layer of small stones is spread along the bottom of the trench to get it ready for the pipes. "I'll get the pipes," shouts Pete. He drives to the site store and picks up some pipes in the front loader.

A pipe is slung from the backhoe, and Pete lowers it carefully into the trench. He cannot see inside the trench very clearly, so Mike signals to him. "Left, left... right. Back a little. Now down... that's it!"

The digger is starting another job when suddenly
oil spurts from a hose on the backhoe arm. "Oh no!"
groans Pete. He turns off the engine, but the hose
has split and the cab window is splattered with
oil. Pete tells Ed, who calls the mechanics.

Work stops until the mechanics arrive to put
in a new hose. The digger will soon be due for
maintenance, so the mechanics decide to do it while
they are there. They check all the machinery and the
engine to make sure that everything is working well.

Months pass. The houses are nearly all built, but the digger is still busy. The bumpy ground behind the houses has to be made into backyards. While Pete uses the digger to clear and level the ground, a dump truck brings over a load of topsoil.

The dump truck tips the soil onto the ground, and Pete uses the front loader to spread it. While the dump truck goes to get another load, the digger moves back and clears another piece of ground. Soon the new yards are ready.

The housing development is finished now, but a new site is beginning close by. Pete can drive the digger straight there. He puts one spare bucket in the backhoe and the other in the front loader, with cans of oil and fuel for the digger.

Pete fastens a flashing yellow light to the top
of the cab to warn other drivers that the digger
can only move slowly. Then he waves good-bye
and roars off. They are on their way to the
next construction site.

Some Special Words

Banksman The person who works on the ground alongside the digger, helping the driver and shoveling bits of loose ground.

Breaker A drill that can be attached to the digger to break up large lumps of rock or concrete.

Concrete Made by mixing sand, gravel, and water with cement. As it dries, it forms a hard, strong block.

Drains Pipes that carry away waste water.

Foreman The person in charge of a construction site.

Foundations Walls or pillars built into the ground to be the base of a building.

Hose A narrow tube made of rubber or plastic.

Housing development A group of houses built together.

Maintenance A regular check that makes sure all the parts of a machine are working well.

Mechanic A person who looks after and fixes machinery.

Ramp A slope that leads from one level to another.

Topsoil The top layer of the ground, in which plants grow.

Trench A long, narrow ditch.

Site store A place on a construction site where bricks, pipes, and other equipment are stored.

THE STORY OF A
TRACTOR

The tractor in this story is a John Deere 2850. It is used all year round on the farm to pull heavy carts and machinery.

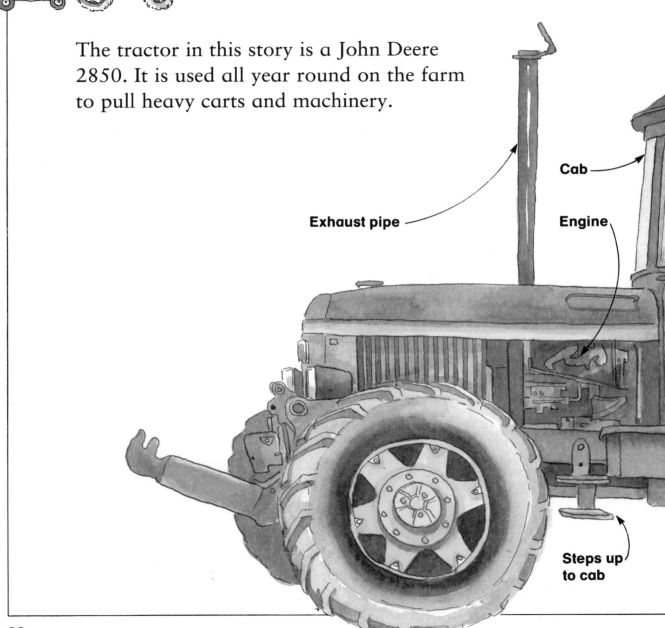

Exhaust pipe

Cab

Engine

Steps up to cab

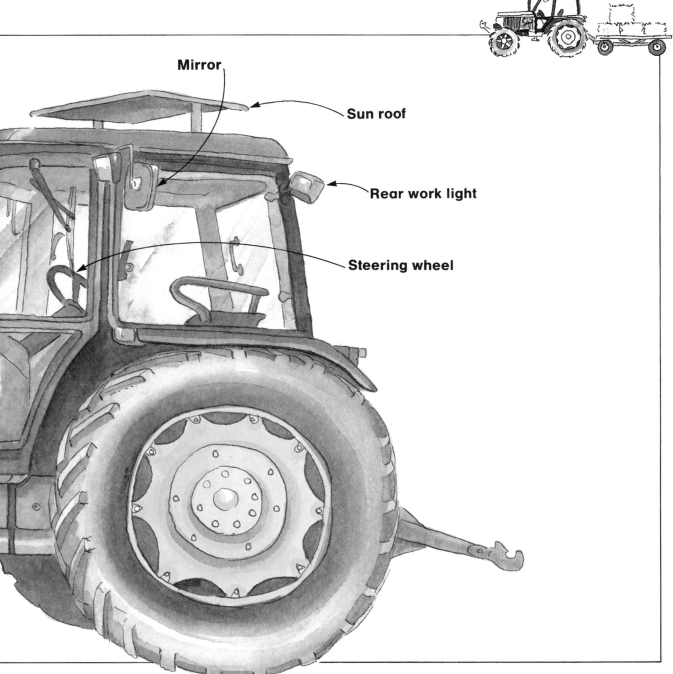

Mirror

Sun roof

Rear work light

Steering wheel

One cold morning, the tractor is in the farmyard.
Joe, the farmer, arrives. He climbs up the steep
steps into the cab and starts the engine. As the
engine splutters to life, the cat jumps with fright
and runs away. Then Joe hooks on the trailer.

He drives to the barn, where he loads up with two
bags of pig feed and some bales of straw. It is winter,
and the pigs need the straw to keep them warm at
night. Joe climbs back up into the cab, turns on
the heater, and sets off down the lane.

The lane is so bumpy that the trailer rattles and lurches behind the tractor. Joe reaches the pigs' field and climbs down to open the gate. As he drives the tractor into the field, its wheels sink down into the thick mud.

Joe pushes down the accelerator. Mud splatters out. Then the big wheels begin to grip, and the tractor slowly moves forward. The pigs are hungry, so first Joe fills their troughs with feed, then he unloads the new straw and spreads it in their pens.

As spring comes, the grass begins to grow again.
Soon it is long enough to be cut, so Joe hooks the
mower to the back of the tractor and joins up the
power wires. When he reaches the field, he pulls a
lever in the cab to make the mower cut the grass.

Joe leaves the cut grass on the ground to dry in the sunshine. After a few days, the grass is turned over, and it slowly turns into hay. Now Joe hooks the big baling machine to the tractor and tows it out to the hay field.

Joe works the lever to make the baling machine pick up the hay from the ground and press it into square bales. Then the machine ties each bale with string and pushes it out the back. But that afternoon the sky clouds over, and a cold wind starts to blow.

"Looks like rain," says Joe to Cathy and Jim.
They hurry to load the bales onto the trailer, and
Cathy's tractor pulls a load to the barn. It is already
dark and raining by the time the last heavy load
is in. "We've just made it!" says Cathy.

The hay is safely in, but millions of aphids have hatched in the good weather to eat the growing wheat. Joe must spray them with insecticide before they spoil the crop. He pours water and insecticide into the sprayer and then joins it to the tractor.

When he reaches the wheat field, he unfolds the
boom arms. He drives through the crop and lets
a fine spray of insecticide fall on the aphids.

It is almost the end of summer now, and Joe's wheat is ripe. He cuts it with a combine harvester.

The combine separates the grain from the stalks and chaff, and pushes the grain through a spout into a trailer. The stalks and chaff fall from the back of the combine onto the field.

The tractor takes the trailerful of grain to the farm and tips it into a big hopper to dry.

When the combine has finished, the baling machine makes the straw that is left in the field into bales.

The weeks pass and the fall comes. All the straw
has been baled and stored for the animals to use
during the winter. Now it is time to plow the
fields, ready to sow a new crop for next year.

As Joe pulls the plow, its blades cut into the ground and turn over the soil. The roots of this year's plants are pulled out and mixed in with the soil. Soon the yellow field has changed to brown.

The next morning, Joe fastens a drill to the back of
the tractor. He fills the seed box with seeds and fertilizer,
which will help the seeds grow. The drill scratches
shallow lines in the ground, and the seeds and
fertilizer trickle into them.

The harrow at the back rakes the soil over the seeds.
"I hope these grow into a crop as good as this
year's," thinks Joe.

43

It is winter again. There is not much work for the tractor to do now, so Joe decides to clean it and service the engine. He washes it with water from a hose and scrapes off the mud that has collected under the engine.

He checks and cleans different parts of the engine. Then he drains out the old, dirty oil and pours in new oil. "This old tractor should keep going for many years to come," thinks Joe, as he gets it ready for another busy spring and summer.

Some Special Words

Accelerator The lever that makes the engine run faster or slower.

Bales Large packages. A baling machine presses hay or straw into large, square packages.

Boom arms Long arms on a sprayer that reach out from each side.

Chaff What is left of the ears of wheat when the grain has been taken out.

Combine harvester A machine that cuts wheat and separates the grain from the stalks and chaff.

Drill A machine for planting seeds.

Fertilizer Food for plants to help them grow.

Harrow A machine like a rake that covers seeds with soil.

Hay Dried grass.

Hopper An open box in which grain is stored.

Insecticide Chemicals for killing insects.

Mower A machine that cuts grass.

Plow A machine that digs up and turns over the soil.

Power wires Wires that carry electricity.

Service A regular check that makes sure all the parts of an engine are working well.

Straw Stalks of wheat after it has been cut.

THE STORY OF A
TUGBOAT

The tugboat in this story is a river tug. It pulls ships up and down the deep-water channels in the river and helps them reach the docks safely.

Fire guns

Galley

Towrope

Engine room

Propeller

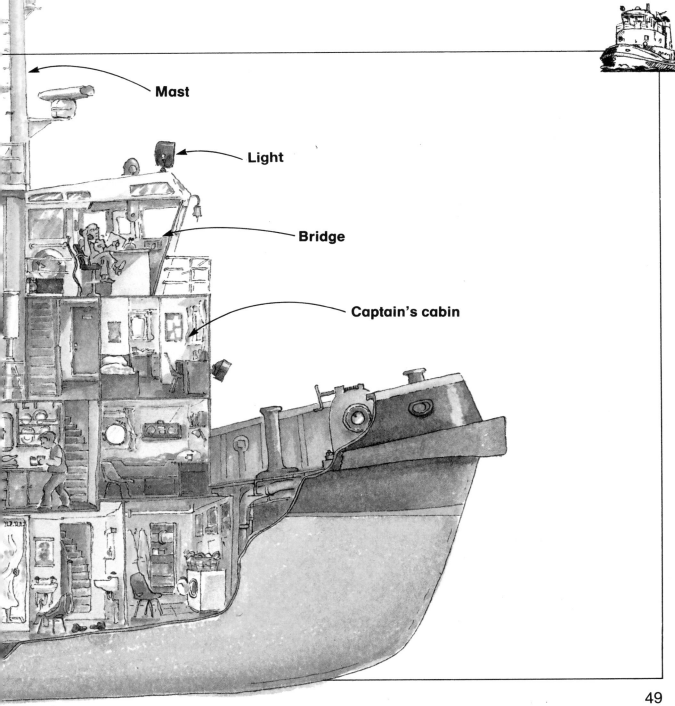

Mast

Light

Bridge

Captain's cabin

49

It is early morning on the river, and only the cries of the seabirds break the silence. At the mouth of the river, several big ships are waiting to sail up to the docks. It is low tide now, so the river is not yet deep enough for them to sail.

The new crew has just taken over the *Jupiter*, a tugboat moored in the river. While they wait for the tide to come in, they get to work cleaning and painting the tug. In the engine room, Paul and John, the engineers, clean the engine.

A few hours later, it is nearly high tide. A big ship steams slowly up the river, and a launch and two tugs go to meet it. The pilot climbs from the launch onto the ship. The tugs will help him steer the ship up the river and into the docks. He radios to *Jupiter*, "Pilot to *Jupiter*, take the port side."

Dave, a deckhand on the *Jupiter*, throws a light rope onto the left side of the ship. The sailors on the ship use this line to pull up the tug's thick, strong rope, which will tow them up the river.

The second tug, *Saturn*, throws a rope onto the other side of the ship. "Slow speed ahead," the pilot radios to the tugs. As the powerful engines move the tugs forward, the ropes tighten. Slowly, the tugs pull the ship up the river.

The pilot wants to turn the ship to face down the river before it reaches the docks. So *Saturn* and *Jupiter* both pull the ship's bow around, and the ship's captain uses the ship's engines to help it turn. The tugs then pull the ship toward the docks.

The ship is nearly docked. A sailor on the ship
unloops the tug's rope, and Dave, Chris, and Steve
haul it back onto the tug.

Then the two tugs nudge the ship until it is closer to the docks. The mooring ropes are tied to hold the ship in place. "Job completed," Ken, the captain, radios to the control room. From the tug company's office, the control room tells him the tug's next job.

The tug steams down the river to collect another ship waiting in the dock. In the galley, Chris quickly makes lunch for the crew. But the tug suddenly shudders as it hits something in the water.

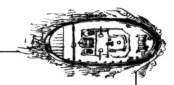

Ken signals to Paul to stop the engine, and the others
run to the deck to see if the propellers are caught.
If they are, the crew will have to wait for a diver
to free them. This time they are lucky. Ken signals
"full astern," and as the tug goes backward, an
old car tire bobs to the surface. The crew cheers!

A few hours later, the control room radios to Ken that a ship is on fire farther down the river. "We're on our way," Ken replies.

As the tug rushes to help, Dave connects the fire hoses to the side of the tug.

Steve and Chris climb the steep ladders to the
fire guns on the mast.

When they reach the ship, Paul starts the pump
in the engine room, and Dave passes the hoses
to the sailors on the ship.

Then Dave climbs down into the ship with a hose so he can fight the fire inside. Steve and Chris use the fire guns to spray water on the burning deck.

Other tugs rush to the rescue too, and they all work together to put out the flames. Two hours later, the fire is out.

While two tugs tow the damaged ship to the docks, *Jupiter* stays behind to clean up some oil that has spilled from the ship's engines. The crew decides to spray the oil with detergent to break it up.

Steve and Chris attach sprays to the ends of two long arms that fold out over the sides of the tug. Dave slings a wooden boom over the stern to help break up the oil. Soon the oil is cleaned up.

Evening comes, and the tide is high again. The tug
is pulling another ship up to the docks. Although it
is dark, Ken can easily see where to go, because the
river's deep-water channels are marked by buoys,
each with a flashing light on top.

Soon they reach the docks and help moor the
ship. The tide is going out again, and the crew can
rest at last. They will be glad to see the launch when
it comes to get them early in the morning, bringing
the next day's crew.

Some Special Words

Boom A slatted, wooden float.

Bow The front of a ship or boat.

Bridge A ship's control room.

Buoy A float in a harbor or river that marks the deep-water channels.

Deckhand A sailor who works mostly on deck.

Deep-water channels The deepest parts of a river where ships can go safely.

Detergent Chemicals that help break up oil and grease.

Docks A place in a harbor or river where ships are loaded and unloaded.

Engineer The person who works the engines.

Full astern Go backward as fast as possible.

Galley A ship's kitchen.

Harbor A sheltered area of water for ships.

Launch A small boat used to carry people between the shore and a ship.

Moored Tied up.

Pilot The person who guides a ship into a harbor or up a river.

Port Sailor's word for left.

Slow speed ahead Go forward slowly.

Starboard Sailor's word for right.

Stern The back of a ship.

THE STORY OF A
HELICOPTER

The helicopter in this story is a Sea King. Different kinds of helicopters are used for different work. Sea Kings are often used for rescues from the air.

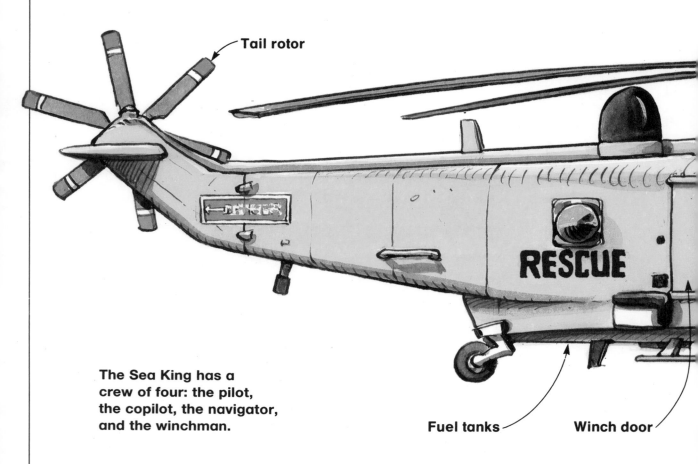

Tail rotor

RESCUE

The Sea King has a crew of four: the pilot, the copilot, the navigator, and the winchman.

Fuel tanks

Winch door

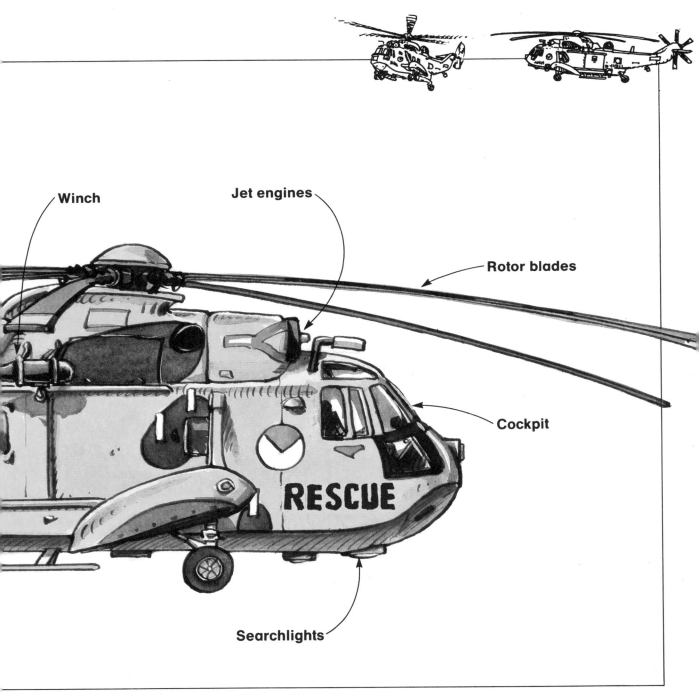

Winch

Jet engines

Rotor blades

Cockpit

RESCUE

Searchlights

71

The helicopter waits at the airbase for an emergency
call. It is ready to fly at a moment's notice to rescue
people from cliffs or mountains, from ships or the sea.
But this morning there are no calls, so the four crew
members work in the office.

After lunch, the crew puts on helmets, life jackets, and gloves and goes out to the helicopter. They fly every day to practice different kinds of rescues. Today John will come with them so they can practice lifting him from a life raft in the ocean.

Gary, the pilot, starts the engines, and the rotor blades whirl. He pulls a lever to make the helicopter rise slowly. Then Gary steers it toward the ocean. The engines are so noisy that the crew uses microphones in their helmets to talk to each other.

"Here's a clear patch of water where we can lower John," says Chris, the copilot. John fastens the life raft on his back and then clips himself to the hook at the end of the winch cable. Steve opens the winch door and lowers him down slowly.

When John reaches the water, he unhooks himself.
He quickly unpacks the life raft and inflates it. Now
it is Mike's turn. Steve pulls the winch cable back
in and fastens the hook to Mike's harness.

Steve lowers Mike toward the water. When Mike lands
on the life raft, he fastens John to his harness and
signals to Steve in the helicopter hovering above.
Steve then hauls the two men up together.

They practice rescuing John several more times before they pull the life raft into the helicopter and fly back to the airbase. "Sea King 166, you can land now," says Air Traffic Control to Gary on the radio. Gary brings the helicopter slowly down.

As soon as the helicopter lands, the ground crew goes to work. They wash the salt water off the winch cable and oil it to keep it from rusting. They refill the fuel tanks and check the engines. Soon the helicopter is ready to fly again.

Suddenly the red emergency telephone rings. Chris answers it. "A sailor has been badly hurt. He has to go to the hospital at once." The Coast Guard tells Chris where to find the ship.

It is evening and getting colder. All the crew members quickly put on immersion suits to keep them warm.

They run to the helicopter, start the engines, and check that they have everything they need.

Seven minutes after the telephone rang, the helicopter takes off. Chris taps the ship's position into the computer. Now Gary can use the compass to find the ship.

It is getting dark, so Gary and Chris cannot see
clearly outside. The compass shows them which
way to go. Steve watches for the ship on the radar
screen. "Ship close by on right," Steve says. Chris
turns on the searchlights, and Steve opens
the winch door.

While the helicopter circles, Steve and Mike peer down into the beam of light. "There it is, 100 yards on the right!" shouts Mike. Chris radios to the Coast Guard that they have found the ship.

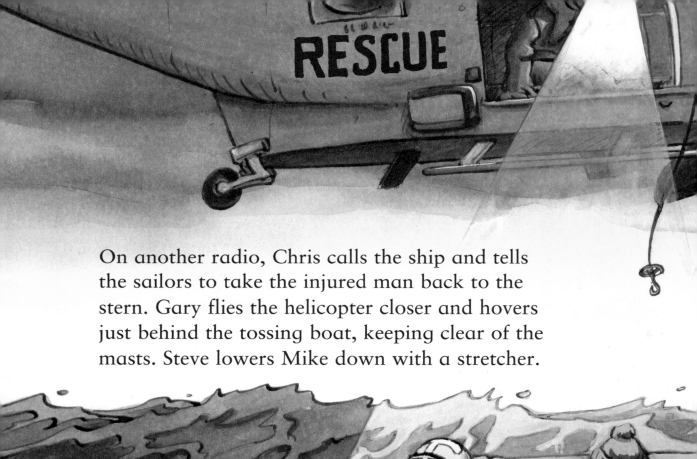

On another radio, Chris calls the ship and tells the sailors to take the injured man back to the stern. Gary flies the helicopter closer and hovers just behind the tossing boat, keeping clear of the masts. Steve lowers Mike down with a stretcher.

Gary brings the helicopter forward a little, and Mike's feet touch the deck. He fastens the injured man to the stretcher. Steve winches them up together. "Winchman and casualty on board," reports Steve as he shuts the winch door.

Gary turns the helicopter back toward land while Chris radios the Coast Guard. They decide that the helicopter should go to the nearest hospital. A space is cleared in the hospital parking lot so the helicopter can land. Two cars light the landing spot.

The police and a fire engine wait close by in case there is an accident. As the helicopter gets nearer, Gary turns on the searchlights. He gently brings the helicopter down to land, and the injured sailor is rushed into the hospital.

The helicopter takes off and flies back to the airbase. At once the ground crew gets it ready to fly again, then they tow it into the shelter of the hangar for the night.

There are no more emergency calls that night, so both the air and ground crews get some sleep. Early the next morning, the helicopter is towed onto the runway, ready for that day's crews to take over.

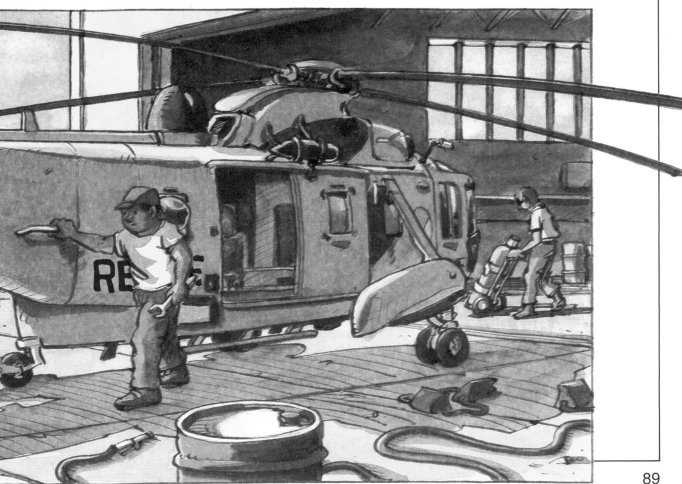

Some Special Words

Air Traffic Control A group of people who control where and when aircraft can fly.

Airbase A place where aircraft can take off and land.

Cable Strong wire rope.

Casualty An injured person.

Coast Guard A group of people who watch over a stretch of coast.

Compass An instrument that shows which direction you are going.

Hangar A large building in which aircraft are kept.

Harness Straps that go around a person and can then fasten onto something else.

Immersion suit Overalls that a crew member wears over a flying suit to keep warm and dry.

Life jacket A jacket filled with air that keeps a person afloat in the water.

Life raft A raft that cannot sink. It is often made of wood or plastic filled with air.

Radar An instrument that detects ships and large objects and shows their location on a screen.

Stern The back of a ship.

Winch A device that pulls in and lets out rope using a wheel.

Winchman A person who is lowered by winch to rescue a casualty.

THE STORY OF A
JUMBO JET

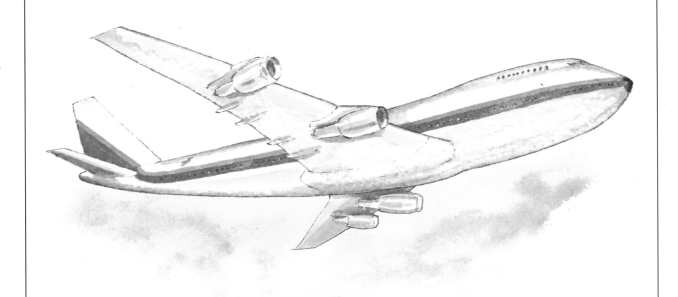

The plane in this story is a Boeing 747.
It can carry over 400 passengers and
is the biggest passenger aircraft.

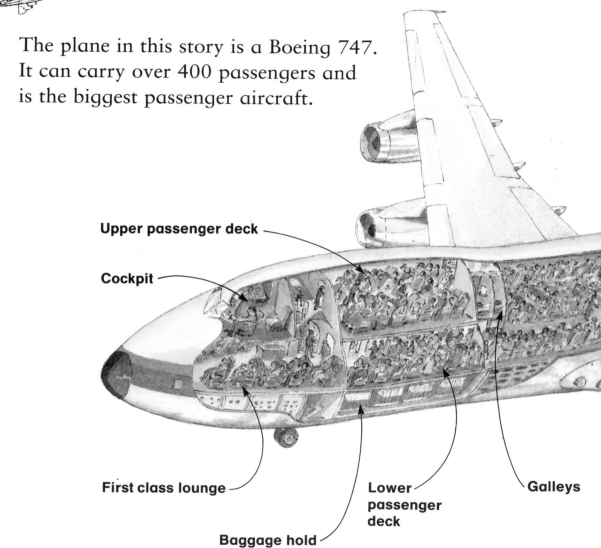

Upper passenger deck

Cockpit

First class lounge

Baggage hold

Lower passenger deck

Galleys

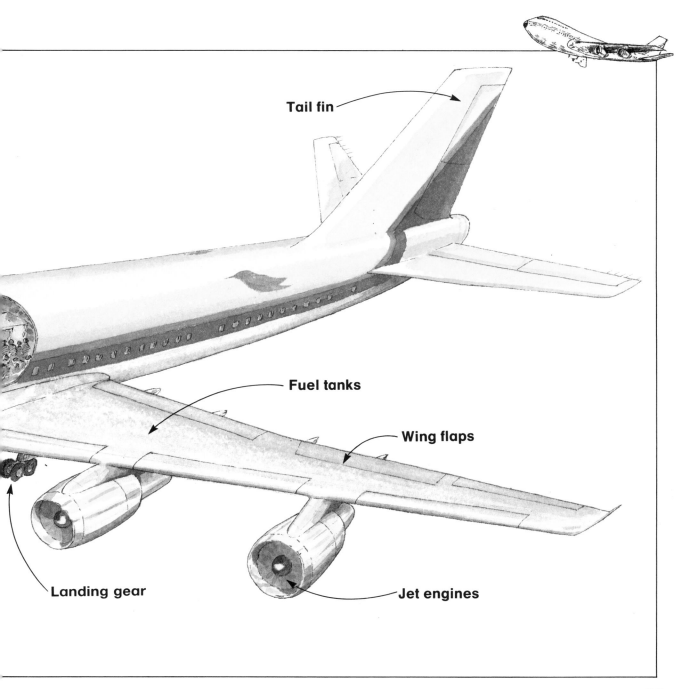

Tail fin

Fuel tanks

Wing flaps

Landing gear

Jet engines

The jumbo jet taxis out to the runway at an airport in New York. It is morning, and many planes are taking off and landing. Tom, the pilot of the jumbo jet, hears a message from the control tower on his earphones: "Bluebird 202 cleared for takeoff."

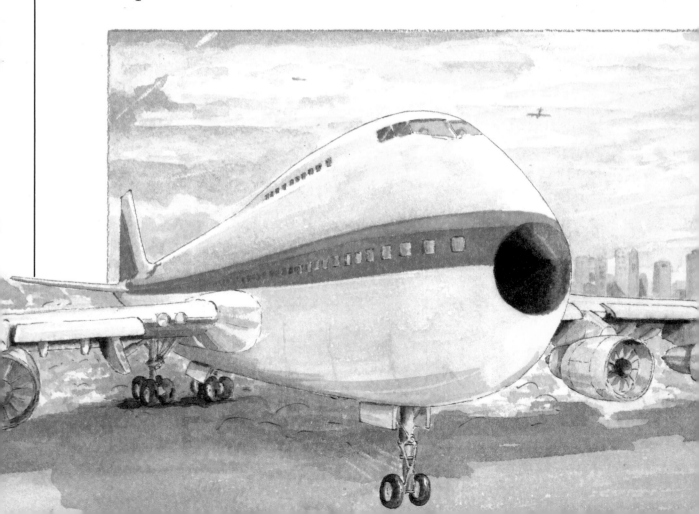

Tom pushes the throttle forward. The jet engines roar as they build up power, and the jumbo jet starts to speed down the runway. Kate, the copilot, calls out the plane's speed to Tom, "100 knots, 120, 130...takeoff!"

Tom pulls the control column, and the heavy plane
rises smoothly into the air. He moves another lever
to pull up the landing gear, then the plane climbs
high above the ground. Some of the passengers
look out of the jumbo jet's windows.

They have left the airport far below. Even
New York's skyscrapers now look like matchboxes.
The plane climbs higher and higher, up through the
clouds and into the sunshine above them. The
jumbo jet is on its way to London.

Air Traffic Control tells Kate how high to fly and which route to take. She taps this into the plane's computer. Now Tom switches over to automatic pilot so the plane will fly itself. Tom, Kate, and John, the engineer, watch the dials to make sure that everything is working properly.

Then Kate sees a black blob on the weather radar.
"Thunderstorm ahead," she says. Tom taps a new
route into the computer so the jumbo jet will
avoid the storm.

Meanwhile, the passengers are settling down in their seats, ready for the long journey ahead. It will take the jumbo jet about six hours to fly to London. Maria and the rest of the cabin crew use the plane's ovens to heat up a meal for everyone.

Maria loads her trolley with food and takes it to
the passengers. "Just look at those black clouds,"
one boy says to Maria. "Yes," she replies,
"there's a big thunderstorm going on over
there, but we're going around it."

The plane has been flying for five hours when John notices that one of the dials has lit up. He checks the other dials and sees that the oil pressure is low. "Engine number three is overheating," he says to Tom.

Tom takes that engine off automatic control. He makes it work more slowly so that it quickly cools down. "I'll report it to the ground crew when we land," he says. The jumbo jet flies smoothly on, and the sun begins to set. They will soon reach the London airport.

When the plane starts its landing, Maria checks
that all the passengers have fastened their seat belts.
Radio instruments guide Tom to the runway and
show him how high the plane should be. The jumbo
jet gets lower and lower, and soon Tom can see
the lights on the runway ahead.

Tom lowers the flaps on the wings to help the plane slow down. "Bluebird 202 cleared to land," radios the control tower. Tom lowers the wheels. The plane skims over a bar of green lights, and a few seconds later, the wheels touch the ground. Quickly, Tom uses the brakes and engines to stop the plane.

The jumbo jet taxis to the passenger buildings,
and Tom stops the engines.

An air bridge is attached to the door of the plane
so the passengers walk straight into the building.

Baggage handlers unload the suitcases, and cleaners arrive to clean the inside of the plane.

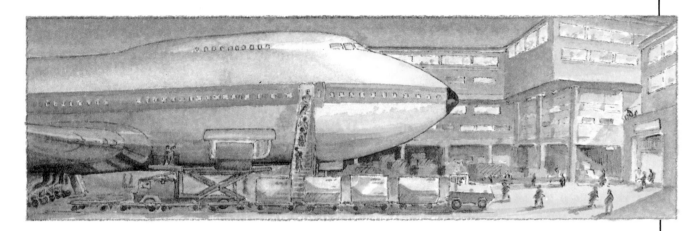

A fuel tanker refills the plane's tanks with fuel from an underground tank.

Tom tells Lee, the ground engineer, about the
problem with engine number three. "I'll take a look
at it right away," says Lee. Tom then joins the air
crew, who are going off to rest.

Lee and another engineer are lifted up to the engine.
They take off part of the cowling and look inside
using special instruments. "We'll have to change
this engine," says Lee.

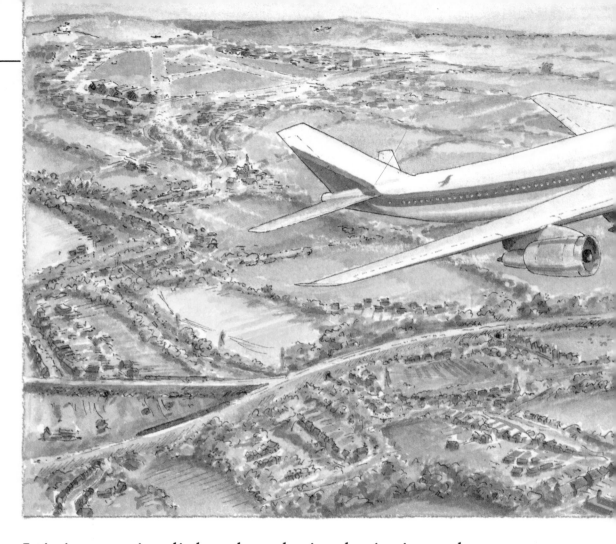

It is just getting light when the jumbo jet is ready
to fly again. The passengers and luggage come on
board while the new crew checks that everything
is working smoothly. Then Dan, the new pilot,
tells the steward to close and lock the doors.

The bridge is taken away, and Dan starts the engines.
At the end of the runway, Dan lowers the wing flaps
so they will help the plane lift up into the air. The
message comes over the radio that they are cleared
for takeoff. Next stop, Jamaica!

Some Special Words

Air bridge A large passageway that passengers walk through to get on and off the plane.

Automatic pilot An instrument that keeps a plane flying at a set height, direction, and speed.

Control column A lever that makes a plane fly higher or lower.

Control tower A building at an airport with computers, radar, and people working in Air Traffic Control.

Cowling The outer covering of a plane's engine.

Flaps Parts of the wings that can be moved to help control the plane's speed.

Landing gear The wheels and other parts that support the plane on the ground.

Oil pressure This shows if the oil is flowing around the engine to keep it working well.

Radar An instrument that detects large objects and shows them on a screen.

Steward/Stewardess A person who looks after the passengers during a flight.

Taxi A plane taxis when it moves along the ground on its wheels.

Throttle A lever that increases or decreases the power of the engines.